MISCELLANEOUS, TENDER

Susanna Styve

ACKNOWLEDGMENTS

Walt Whitman, "Song of Myself," Section 28, lines 1-2, *The Essential Whitman* (Galahad Books, 1992).

Naomi Shihab Nye, "Remembered," *Words Under the Words* (Eighth Mountain Press, 1995).

My heartfelt thanks to all the members of the Laurel Poetry Collective, with special thanks to my friend and fellow dog lover, Su Smallen; a special message of gratitude for Deborah Keenan and Roseann Lloyd—their love and enthusiasm for poetry is both inspirational and infectious. A final thank you to my husband, Arthur Johnson, and the dogs that surround this book, Angus, McEnroe, and Sally.

© 2003 by Susanna Styve
All rights reserved

ISBN 0-9728934-4-X
Library of Congress Catalog Card Number applied for.

Printed in the United States of America

Published by LAUREL POETRY COLLECTIVE,
1168 Laurel Avenue, St. Paul, MN 55104
www.laurelpoetry.com

Book design by Sylvia Ruud

For my mother, my immutable island in rough seas;

And, for my father, whose eyes I will always share;

And, for my husband, who I would choose over and over again.

CONTENTS

Avant-Propos: It Is My Job   9

I. ONES

Only Child   13
Only Child—Protection   14
Only Child, Last Day of Kindergarten   15
Only Child, First Day of First Grade   16
Only Child, Summer   17
Only Child, Charlie's Restaurant, Last Day of Business   18
Only Child, Golf   19
Only Child, German Cup   20
Only Child, Now   21
Only Child, Her Sickness   22

II. TWOS

Love Stories   25
Love Story One, Part Two   26
Love Story One   27

Mother, Beacon	28
Mother	29
Mother, at Home	30
Daughter	31
Daughter, at Home	32
Daughter, Her Block	33
Daughter and Her Changing World	34
Mother, Horizontal	35
Daughter, in Love at Twenty-Seven	36
Mother, in Love at Sixty	37
Family Dog	38
Mother, with Dog	39
Daughter, She Puts Her on a Plane	40
Mother and Daughter Plan a Wedding	41
Mother, on Her Daughter's 28th Birthday	42
Daughter, on an Edge	43
Daughter, God	44
Daughter, Sunday	45
Granddaughter, Improvisation	46
Daughter, Imagining Father, Heaven	47
Daughter, Calm Seas	48
Daughter, on Her 28th Birthday	49

III. SINGULARS

A Dog Remembers, as Pup	53
Thoughts on Home, Musings from a Runaway Dog	54
A Dog Thinks in Reverie	55

A Dog, in Florida	56
A Dog in Dreams	57
How I Remember	58
The Last Great Thing	60
Three Years Mourning	61
A Dream of Men	62
Future	63
For Two	64
Today	65

It Is My Job

> Is this then a touch? quivering me to a new identity,
> Flames and ether making a rush for my veins
> —Walt Whitman, from "Song of Myself" (28)

It is my job to be more than my life,
    to be greater than God, as we find him most often tucked snug
in lessons, rules, knotted up in our fear,
    holding our plague of reins

    as we horses in full throttle, galloping towards cliffs,
galloping for the pure joy of manes and muscle
bend space to accommodate our large bodies,
    rather than folding
        beneath our own weight.

What is more frightening than to be denied the cliff?

Today, it is my job to be a horse in full gait.

It is my job.
    I see fields of clover and lean horses on cold,
stark days with steam thrusting itself from their nostrils.
        They are burning with need, with need not desire.

    It is my job to run;
to be one and singular,
        God-like,

and this various.

ONES

Only Child

We wanted two. But two just wasn't our number. We had one that kept both failure and success in her cup. We monitored too closely. We only had one try.

Only Child—Protection

Father tried to protect mother and daughter from pain of all kinds; mother and daughter protected father from everything that would make him cry out irate; daughter protected mother from father's moodiness acting as a buffer; and mother protected daughter by always standing close to every door to every room she entered alone.

Only Child, Last Day of Kindergarten

What would become ritual—bathtub requiems on the last day of each school year. She rides her yellow banana home, legs sputtering her there like *Chitty-Chitty Bang-Bang*. She's on the verge, wanting to be wet and clean of this new remorse. The yellow banana is dropped to the gravel. Upstairs, she is submerged in rusty well water. The mother, not quite hearing the daughter go up, goes upstairs anyway. *Whatever is the matter?* The daughter is deep in the bathtub sobbing over time, how it owns us all. At six, the daughter knows kindergarten is behind her. At six she knows that nothing will ever be the same again. Nothing ever will be the same again.

Only Child, First Day of First Grade

It will take twenty stickers, one-a-day for twenty school days, to get this girl to stop crying for her mother in the morning hours before reading time.

Only Child, Summer

She hits a tennis ball against the cedar garage. She keeps score between herself. Eventually, she gets pretty good at tennis. At ten, she shirks boys and makeup and the telephone for her sport. She learns how to play against other people.

Only Child, Charlie's Restaurant, Last Day of Business

Fancy steak houses, tapas bars, the only child always gets an invite. She orders filet mignon, medium rare, as she's been taught. At twelve, she's bored, slumping over her food, over the table. *You had such good manners at six. What happened?* She slides down the booth, under the table, to her familiar sanctuary. Curls up and sleeps at feet she'd recognize anywhere. She's slept under tables in many cities. The servers all giggle at her play of nostalgia. They've watched her for years. Charlie, big and Greek, brings her a signature snifter from the bar. "A token," he says, "for your Shirley Temples." She'll keep it stowed away in her jacket, and then in a drawer, and then in her dorm room, and then in a series of apartments, and then in the crystal cabinet of her house.

Only Child, Golf

Wind's been stymied with sun and fever heat isn't pulling down on her shoulders. Golf connects her to her body, connects her body to the motion of the inanimate. She sometimes prays here, on the first green, on the eighth tee. Not for things other than peace, the quietness that inhabits only the smallest corners of the world. She prays for all creatures: the geese that idle on the fairway of watery holes; the worm pulled by an awkward robin. The only child has a short, controlled backswing—easy, melodic follow-through. Not always perfect, in fact, never.

Only Child, German Cup

She has a favorite cup that her friend brought back from Germany. The cup has her name and a scroll of flowers painted on it, mostly shades of blue, swirls of green. When the grandma comes to live with them, she hides it deep in the cupboard behind the butter dish and high because the grandma is short. Still, every day, the grandma asks for the cup because it's pretty and her favorite, too. Doesn't the grandma see the name on it?

Only Child, Now

She has acquired models of how not to be. Don't whine about how you fear being alone. Value blood, but don't let it become obsession. Don't make little families everywhere.

Only Child, Her Sickness

She forgets other people exist sometimes. It isn't so odious as it may seem. She just puts the rest of the world away in little inconsequential boxes that line her closet. She always returns to take them all back out and ponder, at length, mutual existence. You have to understand, she's spent too much time alone. *Besides*, she thinks, *doesn't everyone exist as their own center?* But it's not a good way to live. She knows this like her own skin. When she's forgotten for too long, the world is strange and unforgiving. It's torture really, to walk down the street and only notice your legs moving through the universe.

TWOS

Love Stories

She supposes they all open with how the parents met, fell in love, and married. She hasn't time for those details, though she knows them like the lines on her mother's face, each river crevasse and sorrow pool. The love stories she needs to talk about are the ones that have followed; how they sustain her like fruit pulp and cage her like some wild beast from an unclaimed jungle.

Love Story One, Part Two

They are a twosome now, two islands linked by an isthmus. The tide washes over their mutual architecture and then wanes to revelation. They breathe separately, but share brother creatures and covet their inheritance. When their third sank, the wind blew hard and tousled their foliage into knotted destruction, but they recovered. The isthmus was a life vein then, kept them as one against the torrent. Now the waters calm to push-pull motions, and they struggle when the fog obscures their view of the other's corner of the sea.

Love Story One

She loved him as root. The other loved him as future. So whose loss was harder? Only now has this become an issue.

Mother, Beacon

Three weeks she's been home and still the little bird thrusting itself daily against the kitchen window. She had to leave John in Florida by the side of the pool. This little bird, a simple black and white swallow, wanting to barn down in her house as though it were still his own. *John, John*, she says one morning. *If that is you, go away. You are making me crazy.*

Mother

She's rediscovered art and the piano. Polonaise in A-flat and the new Abnet watercolor with the angry, round cardinal hanging above the fireplace. Things still aren't easy, there are so many empty spaces to fill and silences to play through. What's amazing to her is how nothing stays orderly now. But, maybe she just notices it all more—the dust, the dirt, the filmy windows. Her daughter always says *Can't you hire someone? Can't you just ask for help?* Losing control at sixty—her daughter doesn't understand this.

Mother, at Home

Actually, she has two homes. One is like a summer camp year round. The other grounds her with its familiar upkeep and proximity to Daughter. The summer camp is more to her liking these days. They travel in packs of three or four, inter-gender, to golf, to tennis, to get ice cream. There is always sun and rainstorm in every day. The dog is sometimes there, sometimes not, and when he is, the summer camp fills with sounds of his dream-kicking. She thinks daily of selling out the Daughter and moving to summer camp full-time.

Daughter

She had two, now she has one. She dotes and frets, but comes by it honestly. Previously, she prided herself on being close with them; now she is going for daughter of the year. She wants banners and trophies and glass sculptures saying so. Daughtering could be her full-time job; bitching about it, her hobby. She is walking down a path so dense with moss and fog that her feet have disappeared. She wants to be free of this path, but forgets to look where she's going.

Daughter, at Home

She has two homes, too. One she owns and the other she is expected to love more than the one she owns. She never has quite loved the latter correctly. Always, it's been too remote, too quiet, too full of stifle. The deer used to spy through the windows, then run deep into woods when she'd catch their wide eyes, and they weren't predatory. She was the predatory one there. Wanted to make her parents bleed for having only one. Somehow she thought she would love them less fiercely. Her new home is full of flowers, dust, noise. She budgets for the flowers. Her new home is still less work than the old. The old one should just become a museum.

Daughter, Her Block

She's just been to the corner grocer for a pack of Camels, 1% milk, and a *People*. It's early autumn; the trees are beginning to lighten their load and she's starting to crave hot meals. On the front stoop of the house exactly three hundred yards south of her own, a mother and daughter sit. The mother has her arm around the young girl, sixteen at most. School just started. It must be boy troubles, friend troubles. Right outside her front door, a father is circling on his hand-fashioned, low-rider bike while his son pumps to keep up on his blade scooter. Tonight, on her block, all these small tendernesses; she is happy to be alive.

Daughter and Her Changing World

She buys a house; her mother has a heart attack. A real one. For each action, some arbitrary reaction, but she swears it was her house. If only, if only she'd rented for one more stupid year of the calendar. But then, she knows this is irrational. It's a lot like panic; her throat grabs at itself and her chest thunders like a furious, vendetta-driven train. But there is no discernible vendetta, is there? What silly girl could be so vain as to think the ether of the universe noticed her small corner of living? But it can feel like that sometimes, can't it? We buy houses; our parents fall from their tall, vine-covered towers. Nothing is stasis; it's amazing the word even exists.

Mother, Horizontal

She was lying flat but smiling. She had cracked some joke about the EMT seconding as a stand-up comedian. Her color was good, not cyanotic. (The daughter had expected ashen. And didn't she deserve ashen to complete the melodrama of two hours waiting?) But the daughter got full pink and smiling. Pupils responsive, chest pains, well, yes, but not crushing. She was horizontal and aching all over the bed.

Daughter, in Love at Twenty-Seven

They share a house. They share most everything now. Still, it's new and they find corners for stealing away together. They are working on kinesics; left head tilt always means: "What the fuck are you thinking?" Right arm rests on left shoulder while watching children pump by on their skateboards. They will quit smoking. Neither believes it of themselves, but will do it so the other may live to be ninety. The cat sleeps at the foot of their bed, bites the daughter's toes, reminds the daughter she has people to feed. Suddenly, this keeps her up at night.

Mother, in Love at Sixty

Reason number one it can't work: his name is Bill. For god's sake, he hunts. He has no pets, other than two doting daughters, and his ex-wife is still alive. He's simply not my type. Who wants to get married again, anyway? I'm too old. I go South at the first frost. Plus, he's messy. Men are messy. He could die. Then where would I be?

Family Dog

The family dog is to be visited. He must wait at the old home for the children to come back on holidays, laundry visits, to fix the computer, to introduce their betrotheds, etc. He's to be cried over when the call comes to say that he is dead. He is to represent the past, a token of childhood, a comforting back to scratch when you move home post-heartbreak. This is the role of the family dog.

Mother, with Dog

She drops off the family dog. The mother and her travels, to neither can the daughter say "no." Here, the beloved, clutzy dog with the loose back legs has broken with destiny. The daughter never signed on to dog ownership, never expected to share ninety pounds with her mother. My life was clean, she protests, had a cat and a man in it. Now the cat lives in the basement like some mad rat, and the man runs off to work without goodbyes. The daughter is trapped between the future and the past. She feels utterly interrupted. Somewhere in the Keys her mother floats on a boat.

Daughter, She Puts Her on a Plane

It doesn't matter where the plane goes. Freedom always comes with a chest of molten lead. Don't, anybody, touch her. She doesn't want hands right now. She'd rather read Rimbaud and drift moor-less in self-pity. This kind of heaviness especially hates company. Her nose always itches for three straight days after planes take her mother away. Why should there be guilt over love outside of blood? She knows phone calls every other day will arrive. There will be adjustments like the tedious work of hemlines. Don't they do this every year? Split apart like dangerous atoms, fuse back together like candle wax.

Mother and Daughter Plan a Wedding

They might as well just have a ceremony. The cord is a double-noose knot. They'll both wear cream. (There's no purity in ferocious need.) They'll eat cheesecake. They'll invite everyone. All those third wheels will bounce idly away down both roads. Who could possibly compete with this attachment? No man could put asunder such devotion.

Mother, on Her Daughter's 28th Birthday

Today is the day a mother never forgets. Maybe if there are seven, she has to write them all down. She has one. But this year it got lost somewhere: stuck behind the bathroom vanity, tossed in the south ravine with dead underbrush, left behind on the 17th green with a lonely putter, discarded absentmindedly at a restaurant like an orthodontic retainer. Mothers make these mistakes, don't they? When their lives fill up with themselves. When they find new loves to answer the daily barrage of self-doubtings. Besides, daughters seek new families now, find other guests to fill their birthday parties.

Daughter, on an Edge

Somewhere between panic and her cupboard, she realizes that everyone lives by their own choosing. She reaches in to retrieve that certain wineglass, the one with the scant stem and cavernous bowl. She slips the stem between her third and fourth fingers so the bowl rests warm in her palm. The pinot is cranberry stain and she swirls it the way her lover does. He creates tides with his wine like he created her into mythical perfection. Sadly, she is not perfect. She is caught somewhere between her mother's obligatory blood and his reverie. She can live up to neither. Tonight she is alone with her wine and can breathe.

Daughter, God

She sees lovely things in the dust pillows collecting under the bed, notices how dust huddles en masse, refuses aloneness. She often does too. Her throat closes up, her eyes water, she sneezes five times and nobody is there to hear it. It's funny how she fears being alone most when she's not. Don't leave me, she thinks, but has learned not to say it out loud. Nobody likes desperation, except God. God thrives there, always finds her broken in fever sleep. When she wakes, she's forgotten the whole meeting, but notices dust in motion. Finds it somehow beautiful. Finds strange comfort.

Daughter, Sunday

Mostly her Sundays are about crosswords. Sometimes football. Never shopping. Never church. Walking, maybe, when there are places to reach or a whimpering dog underfoot. This is all restful, she thinks. I rest on Sundays. On Sundays, I fill myself back up. God is a four-letter word. Rest.

Granddaughter, Improvisation

The grandma was dying; it was to be a big lesson. But before the grandma went, she lost her sense of place. The granddaughter spent nights with her, would sit on the floor beside her La-Z-Boy and hum big-band tunes. Once the grandma called her an angel—a white, flossy angel. Once the grandma asked the granddaughter to retrieve her can of Vienna sausages from the kitchen cupboard. The granddaughter could find no Vienna sausages; in fact, she couldn't even find the cupboard that the grandma was speaking of. She found cocktail wieners though, and they ate them until their stomachs were full and salty. The grandma thought they were green beans, had forgotten entirely about the little pink sausages.

Daughter, Imagining Father, Heaven

In addition to dads and moms and sisters, brothers, beloved family pets, she hopes for Shakespeares, Payne Stewarts, Ptolemies. She hopes there are no boundaries, that handshakes between ages and statures are rote truths. She imagines that maybe he's run for some office or is in the business of writing articles of whimsy for the Heaven Gazette. She still thinks in physics because it's what living humans have. She hopes in some cerebral way that such rules don't apply, but can't envision this. She only wants more for him up there than he had here. She knows she asks a lot of her imagination, but it helps her sleep at night when she can't get his face out of her head.

Daughter, Calm Seas

This morning, a new chapter. The dog barks outside wanting to be in. The hairs on her arm feel like cacti needles, prick her to blood. She is dangerous. Their spontaneous tides have flagged to an immutable daily motion. Regularity and calm seas make her lower abdomen churn. How has this gone in the past? It's gone this way: she holds on to high staffs, tries to steer herself and the dead weight of her tow back to roiling waters. She contemplates affairs, but doesn't have them. She creates escape routes, but doesn't use them. She cries out only in privacy and grows publicly demure. What's different this time? He coaxes her into fights, meaningless and silly spats over breakfast, over football. He gets her to cry and announces that he loves her. He asks why she can't be still in warm water. He gathers her up like flotsam and builds minute, tender eddies of laughter between them.

Daughter, on Her 28th Birthday

She thinks how unexpected it is to be this age. How splendid really. And for the first time, it feels like things are beginning, not just changing from one to another. She expects marriage this year; she thinks of long-lived careers. She longs to tell her people that they are her life but she doesn't. Instead she makes arrangements, plans dinners, buys furniture. Everywhere she sees shrines. Her cat paws his way to her lap. He knows she will feed him every day for the rest of his life.

SINGULARS

A Dog Remembers, as Pup

My mother was a piece of ocean glass, beautiful against the sea sand blue and tan. I was her pup among so many, pulling at a teat tattered with pulling. I came by crate and air here, where love was a gift for them to give. *It is okay this way.* I told my mother by dream, for she died when I was two and happy. *I've become a beloved.* I whisper through ocean's dream wake. *A beloved.* Came back faint through glass of surf shells breaking.

Thoughts on Home, Musings from a Runaway Dog

It felt so good to be free for that moment, lifting leg on the second tee box, that plush of short green and the fire ants deterred by rough morning combing machines. For one moment this is all that was—the taste of freedom in my snout, openness of paths and birds and startled armadillos uncomfortable in their little suits of armor. And then, I remember snakes and praying mantis, frantic faces back home and voices cutting through morning. *Gus, Gus, oh god, Gus.* And before I made out that first call I'd turned towards home and those gentle women I father, meeting them barefoot, a half-mile from home, tears and all, robed still, morning-stained, beautiful.

A Dog Thinks in Reverie

We always remember the first. It's the dog way, and I still smell him in untouched corners of carpet, on the shoes she can't seem to part with. My luck and my curse: his being so alive in my nose. Such a thing would kill her. It's a dog's job to shoulder and bully pain away with playfulness, need. I have my own pain I carry in the numbness of my hind legs, the way we used to lie on the L-shaped couch head-to-head, his salty legs after lawn work, his knee for chin rest, spinning the leather recliner Sunday morning newspaper games. It's all like two years blinked, and now I can't help but know there, too, with leash, we'll meet again in the light.

A Dog, in Florida

Somnolent and heavy with salt pork, I melt with my sliding back feet into the geriatric world of Florida. When we pass on the streets, they favoring one hip or knee, and me, with no feeling in back and slipping. They nod knowingly, my tragedy somehow more pitiful. But you too, my cripple friends, walk the degenerative timeline of terminal. Don't we all wish not for pity, but for life worth living? Like yours, mine shall be taken. Unlike you, I will one morning awake in heaven at my master's kind hand. And, on that day, shall think, however unfairly, your world is so greatly more cruel than mine.

A Dog in Dreams

In my dreams, I am greatness: the hunter of whitetails, rabbits, deer, the coyotes that howl from the deep woods by night. I run in dreams, hard with kicking and throaty growls. Some nights, light throws over my running body like blankets, tickling my fur and falling over. It is then I know my own beauty. And in morning I wake stiff and exercised, stretch myself out long and then to her bedside to tell of my dreams of greatness. But she sleeps yet, and I stare into her face 'til she wakes.

How I Remember

> When we left he'd say "Don't forget me! You won't forget me now,
> will you?" as if our remembering could lengthen his life.
> I wanted to assure him, there will always be a cabin in our blood
> only you live in. But the need for remembrance silenced me…
> —from "Remembered," by Naomi Shihab Nye,
> *Words Under the Words*

I.

You did not ask to be remembered, did not sit groping your hands together like sticks for desperate fire. Perhaps you did not know the thread that runs between could snap without warning. But there is always warning, we die. And yet, you did not ask to be remembered. Maybe you knew that trees fall as they will and fires burn untended.

II.

One late evening at the kitchen table. You were drunk. I was not. You were earnest; I wanted only sleep. You looked at me, as I suppose a newborn might look at a first face. *Was there fear?* How big things had gotten. Eyes had become watery worlds. Heart mouth grown to a wellspring. We had warred for seven years over all the little nothings that combine into the whole. I'd gone away to school, come back without blessing, then, gone on to find other schools, new beginnings. You'd made a success of yourself long before I came into the world, but now found tedious work of it. You'd grown tired, and I, braver and ambitious. How strange to be having this conversation; Mom upstairs asleep, the dog a pile of gold underfoot. You said something about our minds being so similar, but mine feeling a few steps ahead. My reply was "I love you, Dad," offering only complacent tolerance of your sudden need to bear witness to us. I didn't know you'd die within months, though I knew by instinct you weren't long for my world. Two years before this moment we'd called a cease-fire, found a place to sit quietly alongside. Mom still tells of the first time you saw me as a baby. You poked at my belly and were disappointed that I didn't open my eyes. You tried my finger and I squeezed back. You started in surprise, then, leaned in closer than you had to anything before.

The Last Great Thing

Joe died before I was born, eighteen years before. My dad was eighteen when he went. Joe married my grandma at fifty-two. She was only twenty-three and already a widow. He called her his last great thing, and then they had three children. I guess they all fell under the category of last great thing, too. Joe's own dad died while he was but a few months in the womb; lored to have passed holding a daguerreotype of his dad, dead at twenty-three in the Civil. This strange relic of metal is mine now, come down through these patrilineal lines. I hardly ever look at it, know the image has faded to a charcoal whisper, but the ink sunk so deep that the image etched itself in. I never called my grandpa that, just called him "Joe" or Joseph Vernon Styve. I suppose my children will call my father "John." I suppose that is okay.

Three Years Mourning

I still swear like a sailor, string expletives together as a lapidary does fine gems. I am making a strong go at living, school, the writing thing, work, money, love, you know. I still read Larry McMurtry novels, just finished *Anything for Billy*. Loved it all over again. I can still feel your thumb pressed to that wrinkle line on my forehead when I am in moments of deep worry. I still vote Democrat, wishing you were here to cancel it out. I miss you daily (okay, days go by, but they're few), sometimes still to the point of empty sleeplessness, despair. But I won't end on that word. These days, I prefer the word "Joy."

A Dream of Men

All the men in this room were once or are still mine. They mill awkwardly, in small mindless conversation with one another. My father, three years dead, is at the center, stands oddly pigeon-toed and silent, under a huge chandelier of melting icicles. Maybe it's not a chandelier, but the room is a cave, and he is under a flush of dripping stalactites. He calls the room to order. Things are dripping all around. Water is running, hollow "plinks," "plunks" echo. I do not see myself anywhere in the room. I do see my first love. I see the most recent past, four years of cohabitation, of building false shrines, of learning lessons I never expected would bear any but bitter fruit, of loving and then unloving, of missing but not ever wanting back. My grandfather is in the mix; the one I never knew, met, even saw in a picture, my dad's dad. An uncle that died when I was seven, who played the piano and baseball, laughed a lot and had red hair, stands beside him. All these faces cross my mind on evenings when there is nothing better to do than dabble in idle melancholy. The cave falls silent; my dad has called order. The cave walls and ceiling belt in around this circle of bodies. Heated conversation opens; so orderly these men are in having their say. One at a time they speak; someone is being tested, someone being judged by this quorum. I cannot see to the middle, cannot see who it is being measured.

Future

He is now my husband and we are walking our dog. *Do you remember the first time you met her?* He does because he remembers everything: my white lies, our first house, the time we fixed the toilet with a toothbrush nozzle, our first kiss eight years before the ring. *Wasn't it in Stillwater? I recall that your mother caught me unsuspecting with a huge embrace, nearly knocked me off my feet.* He remembers everything in perfect detail always. What I never told you, my sweet, was that she claimed to have known right then, upon first sight, that you would be my family when the last physical vestiges of our family triumvirate disappeared. I never inquired further, was frightened powerless by the thought of being without her.

For Two

This night, let all cars have two headlights burn simpatico and we a bicycle built strong for just two, the two of us. Handlebars, you hold each side with just room enough for me to feel your steering down and up the roads where houses pair up like socked feet. Let, this night, all alley cats have willing mates to clean and find warmth with. Let all girls have best friends who agree that purple makes their eyes just a little bit greener. And, above all, beyond all, beside all, let me find tomorrow, reading the newspaper, coffee hot with whipped cream and toast and that first new cigarette of the day, that by miraculous light, in all hospitals they died by twos. All couples joined, found themselves by a warm fire. All answers were "yes." All mothers called all daughters to find them safe and in love and full of growing. And, all widows gave over to soft visions in the pleats of their bedroom curtains. Let me find, among the headlines: By all uncanny observation only two shooting stars dashed the August sky last night, two delicate slits through which the heavens rained down.

Today

It was simple. We met at home, walked the three blocks, stood in line listening to the women behind us chatter about church and dead parishioners. I bumped into a poet friend; you were introduced. I vouched for you minutes earlier, then kissed the back of your neck. We voted and walked home. I spent all day thinking about it, stored it under miscellaneous, tender.

SUSANNA STYVE, a native Minnesotan, grew up in Afton, a quaint town on the St. Croix River. This collection was greatly informed by her experiences as an only child in a loving, yet volatile, family of three. She now divides her time between her husband, two dogs, her mother and best friend, and writing. She recently finished an M.F.A. in creative writing from Hamline University. *Miscellaneous, Tender* is her first book.

LAUREL POETRY COLLECTIVE

A gathering of twenty-three poets and graphic artists living in the Twin Cities area, the Laurel Poetry Collective is a self-funded collaboration dedicated to publishing beautiful and affordable books, chapbooks, and broadsides. Started in 2002, its four-year charter is to publish and celebrate, one by one, a book or chapbook by each of its twenty-one poet members. The Laurel members are: Lisa Ann Berg, Teresa Boyer, Annie Breitenbucher, Margot Fortunato Galt, Georgia A. Greeley, Ann Iverson, Mary L. Junge, Deborah Keenan, Joyce Kennedy, Ilze Kļaviņa Mueller, Yvette Nelson, Eileen O'Toole, Kathy Alma Peterson, Regula Russelle, Sylvia Ruud, Tom Ruud, Su Smallen, Susanna Styve, Suzanne Swanson, Nancy M. Walden, Lois Welshons, Pam Wynn, Nolan Zavoral.

For current information about the series—including broadsides, subscriptions, and single copy purchase—visit:

www.laurelpoetry.com

or write:

Laurel Poetry Collective
1168 Laurel Avenue
St. Paul, MN 55104